Landscapes

artist Nathalie Trovato

Edited by Kyla Ryman, Early Childhood Reading Specialist.
Home Grown Books is an artistic and educational collaboration.

city

country

forest

beach

desert

arctic

rainforest

Painting a Landscape

A landscape is a scene that you observe from a single viewpoint. This scene can be real, like your backyard, or imagined like a dream.

For this project, you will need the following:
newspaper, water, crayons, watercolor paint and brushes

1. Find a scene you would like to paint. What makes your scene and viewpoint unique?

2. Use the crayons to draw on the newspaper. Draw shapes and colors that you see or use shapes and colors that describe what you smell, hear or feel.

3. When you are finished, use the watercolor paint to add to your painting.

4. Let your watercolor paint dry and enjoy your beautiful landscape.

Fire

artist Nathalie Trovato

Edited by Kyla Ryman, Early Childhood Reading Specialist.
Home Grown Books is an artistic and educational collaboration.

Volcano erupts.

Fireplace warms.

Rocket launches.

Food grills.

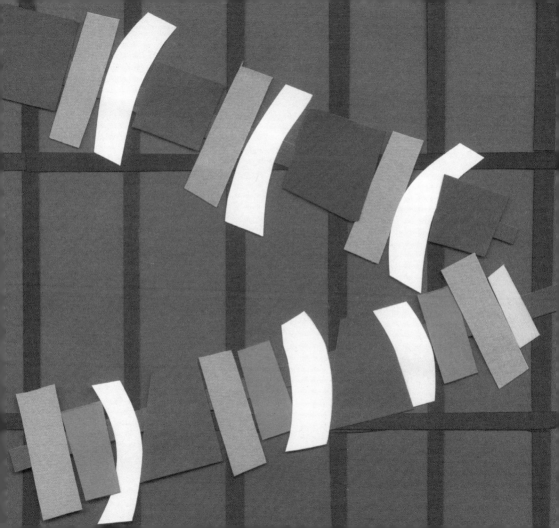

Candles burn.

Lightning strikes.

Fire engine arrives.

Fire Safety

Fire can be beautiful, exciting and useful. It is important that we use fire safety rules whenever we are around flames.

Here are some handy fire safety rules:

- Always have an adult help you when cooking, using matches or building fires.

- Never play with plugs or outlets.

- If you see smoke in a room, lie on the floor on your belly. Crawling under the smoke will keep harmful smoke out of your eyes and lungs.

- Remember, firefighters are our friends and they can help you in an emergency. They wear masks and special clothes to protect themselves in a fire so don't be afraid. Firefighters wear these so that they can do a better job to protect you!

- If you see a fire, tell an adult or call 911.

Written with help from the Georgetown Fire Department in Georgetown, Maine

Earth

artist Nathalie Trovato

Edited by Kyla Ryman, Early Childhood Reading Specialist.
Home Grown Books is an artistic and educational collaboration.

Earth grows grass.
Sheep graze.

Earth is deep.
Rabbits burrow.

Earth makes mud.
Pigs roll.

Earth dries.
Land cracks.

Earth makes clay.
I mold clay.

Earth grows flowers.
I give flowers.

Earth is home.
I live on Earth.

Different Kinds of Earth

Collect samples of earth in containers. Look for dry, hard-packed dirt, loose soil, gravel, sand and clay. After collecting samples, sit down and examine your findings.

For this project you will need the following:
5 empty glass containers and a small shovel

- Can you see differences in earth that was collected from different locations?

- Are your samples dry or moist?

- How many different colors can you find in your samples?

- Pick up a pinch of earth from each sample. How does the earth feel?

- What does earth smell like?

Habitats

artist Nathalie Trovato

Edited by Kyla Ryman, Early Childhood Reading Specialist.
Home Grown Books is an artistic and educational collaboration.

a hut

an apartment

a camper

a stilt house

an igloo

a tipi

a yurt

Your Habitat

A habitat is a place where a particular animal lives. It is the area that surrounds the animal. Most animals build a home, seek out companions and find food in their habitat. In this book, we show human habitats.

Find a piece of paper and draw a picture of your habitat.

Do you share your habitat with other creatures?

Are there any habitats in this book that are similar to yours?

Water

artist Nathalie Trovato

Edited by Kyla Ryman, Early Childhood Reading Specialist.
Home Grown Books is an artistic and educational collaboration.

diving

drinking

fishing

bathing

raining

watering

shipping

Watch how water moves through plants!

For this project, you will need the following:
4 tall clear glasses, 4 trimmed celery stalks, 4 different colors of food coloring, cold water, and a spoon

1. Take 4 tall glasses, and fill each one halfway with water.

2. In each glass add several drops of a different food coloring and stir with the spoon.

3. Put one stalk of celery in each cup.

4. Predict what will change as your celery stalks sit in the colored water overnight.

5. In the morning, check your cups. What has changed? Was your prediction correct?

Air

artist Nathalie Trovato

Edited by Kyla Ryman, Early Childhood Reading Specialist.
Home Grown Books is an artistic and educational collaboration.

I need
fresh air.

I need air
to breathe.

I need air to blow up a balloon.

I need air to
soar over mountains.

I need air to
fly a kite.

I need air to
scuba dive.

I need

clean air.

Use the air you breathe to find calm

Find a quiet place to sit comfortably. Then, sit down with crossed legs.

1. Close your eyes and place your hands on your belly.
2. Feel your belly get big when you breathe in and small when you breathe out.
3. Feel the air as it comes in and out of your nose.
4. Keep breathing in and out for a few minutes or as long as you like.

You can do this alone or with friends and family to calm down and find peace inside.

Offered by Lauren Maples, Director of Bija Kids Yoga in Brooklyn, NY

In My Garden

artist Nathalie Trovato

Edited by Kyla Ryman, Early Childhood Reading Specialist.
Home Grown Books is an artistic and educational collaboration.

seeds in
a pail

water in

a can

a carrot in
the night

poppies in
the field

a worm
in a car

a bird in an
apple tree

a garden in
my window

Grow Your Own Food

Microgreens can be harvested on your windowsill all year long.

To grow your own microgreens, you will need the following:
empty recycled plastic takeaway container with lid, scissors, soil,
seeds and water

1. Place several drain holes in the bottom of the container.
2. Fill the container with soil up to one inch from the top.
3. Sprinkle seeds evenly across the top of the soil.
4. Cover the seeds with a thin layer of soil.
5. Place the lid under your container to catch drips.
6. Add water to your soil until drips emerge from the drainage holes
    at the bottom of your container.
7. Check soil every day and continue to keep soil moist, but not wet,
    as your greens grow.
8. Harvest the microgreens in 1½ to 2 weeks.
9. Add new seeds to the soil as you pick and eat greens for a continual
    source of food!